4/2011
ACPL Laramie, WY
39102000156751
Landau, Elaine.
Are the drums for you? /

WITHDRAWN

D0601958

Sources for Library Materials in FY10
Albany County Public Library

- Cash Gifts
- Public Money
- Donated Items

18%

50%

32%

Albany County
Public Library
Laramie, Wyoming

ARE THE DRUMS FOR YOU?

ELAINE LANDAU

Lerner Publications Company · Minneapolis

Copyright © 2011 by Lerner Publishing Group, Inc.

All rights reserved. International copyright secured. No part of
this book may be reproduced, stored in a retrieval system, or
transmitted in any form or by any means—electronic, mechanical,
photocopying, recording, or otherwise—without the prior written
permission of Lerner Publishing Group, Inc., except for the inclusion
of brief quotations in an acknowledged review.

Lerner Publications Company
A division of Lerner Publishing Group, Inc.
241 First Avenue North
Minneapolis, MN 55401 U.S.A.

Website address: www.lernerbooks.com

Library of Congress Cataloging-in-Publication Data

Landau, Elaine.
    Are the drums for you? / by Elaine Landau.
        p.   cm. — (Ready to make music)
    Includes bibliographical references and index.
    ISBN 978-0-7613-5426-0 (lib. bdg. : alk. paper)
    1. Drum—Juvenile literature 2. Drum set—Juvenile literature
    3. Percussion instruments—Juvenile literature I. Title.
    ML1035.L36 2011
        786.9'19—dc22   2009048971

Manufactured in the United States of America
    1 – DP – 7/15/10

CONTENTS

ONE

THE BEAT GOES ON

Picture this:

You're a drummer in a respected jazz group. The other musicians onstage are taking your music to wild places. Your job is to keep a steady rhythm. Your timing has to be perfect. But there's no need to be nervous. Your performance is wonderful. You're highly skilled and take great pride in your music.

Switch to another scene. You're a drummer with a famous rock band. You're playing to a packed arena. You can sense the energy in the air.

Meg White of the White Stripes rocks out in 2007.

You deliver the beat, and the fans feel it. When the time comes for your drum solo, you rock the house. The crowd is yours.

Can you see yourself in either of these scenes? If you take up the drums, both might be possible. But first, you'll have to practice hard and become an excellent player.

There are lots of great reasons to play the drums. What makes them so terrific? Here's the short list.

SUPER COOL

Drums might be the coolest instruments around! Drummers are always in demand with other musicians. If a group wants to play music with a beat, they'll need someone behind a drum set. Drummers usually have lots of fans too.

EXPRESS YOURSELF

Drums give you a chance to shine as a musician. Drummers can get creative onstage. During a drum solo, a drummer shows fans what he or she can really do. There are no rules for a drum solo. A drummer just plays what he or she feels.

You're part of a family. Family members often have some things in common. Do you have your mother's smile? Your father's nose? And by the way, is that your aunt Alma's red hair?

Instruments are grouped in families too. The drums are part of the percussion family. What do percussion instruments have in common? All of them make a sound when you strike or shake them.

Percussion instruments come in all shapes and sizes. "Every culture has different percussion instruments," explained percussionist Jeff Handel. "Percussion instruments are often developed simply by using whatever happens to be around. It might be dried gourds, tree trunks, or animal skins." Some common percussion instruments in the United States include cymbals, xylophones, triangles—and, of course, drums!

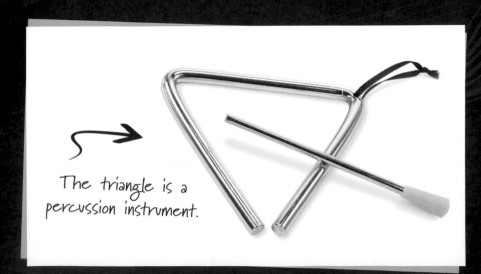

The triangle is a percussion instrument.

CHOO-CHOO!

Drummers have an important job in any musical group. The drummer sets the beat for the whole band. This helps the other band members stay on track. Think of a musical group as a train. There are lots of passengers on the train but just one conductor. The conductor drives the train just as the drummer drives the beat.

WORK IT OUT

Drummers get a workout without going to the gym. You may be sitting on a stool, but your body is always

A drummer's beats keep other musicians on track.

moving to the music. You push your wrist back and forth when you hit a hi-hat (a type of cymbal in a drum set). You stamp your foot to control a bass drum. For this workout, you don't even have to leave your drum set.

Do you see the drums in your future? If so, this book's for you. It's all about drums, percussion, and rhythm. The beat goes on!

CLOSE-UP ON A DRUM SET

The drum set used most often for rock and jazz is known as a five-piece set. As the name suggests, these sets have five main pieces. A bass drum, a snare drum, and three tom-toms are part of a five-piece set. But five-piece sets have other pieces too. These include stands, pedals, and cymbals. Let's take a close-up look at a five-piece set and see how it all comes together.

TOM-TOMS

A drum set's three tom-toms come in different sizes. One tom-tom is usually bigger than the other two. The large tom is placed on the floor. It's held up by small legs. Smaller toms may be attached to a stand on top of the bass drum. These drums are often used to fill in when there's a break in the ongoing drumbeat.

THE SNARE DRUM

The snare drum is a shallow drum with a set of wires called a snare stretched across its bottom. The wires give the drum a hissing sound. The snare drum can be played with a drumstick or a tool called a brush.

THE BASS DRUM

This is the largest drum in a five-piece set. The bass drum is placed on its side on the floor. You don't strike this drum with a drumstick. You play a bass drum by pushing a pedal with your right foot. A stick attached to the pedal hits the drum. The bass drum has a deep, low sound. It thumps out the main pulse of the music's rhythm.

CYMBALS

Drummers use a few different types of cymbals. On a hi-hat, one cymbal faces up while the other faces down. A drummer pushes the two cymbals together with a foot pedal. Most drum sets have at least one crash cymbal. Crash cymbals make a loud crashing sound. Some drum sets also have splash cymbals for a more delicate sound. These cymbals sound like a quick splash of water. Some drum sets use China cymbals too. These sound like crash cymbals but have an even more explosive sound.

TWO

ALL KINDS OF RHYTHMS

Music surrounds us. It's a part of all our lives. You may ride to school with a song in your headphones. Maybe you saw a marching band at a football game. You've probably heard music in elevators and waiting rooms too. And where there's music, you'll often find drums. Just listen for the beat!

ROCK MUSIC

Drums are everywhere in rock music. Rock just wouldn't have the same energy without them. Indeed, many drummers have become famous pounding out the beat for rock bands. One such drummer is Rick Allen of the British hard rock group Def Leppard.

You can hear drum rhythms in many varieties of music.

Allen got his first drum set when he was ten. He made a deal with his parents to get it. He had to take lessons first. He also had to save up to pay for the set. Allen joined Def Leppard in November 1978, when he was just fifteen. By 1983 the band was selling millions of albums. Then tragedy struck.

In 1984 Allen lost his arm in a car accident. His career as a drummer seemed over. But Allen wasn't ready to accept that. He worked with some engineers to design an electronic drum set. This let him use his left foot to play the beats he had played with his left hand. With his new set, Allen's playing sounded great. He became known as the Thunder God. Allen's return to drums may be the greatest comeback story in rock and roll.

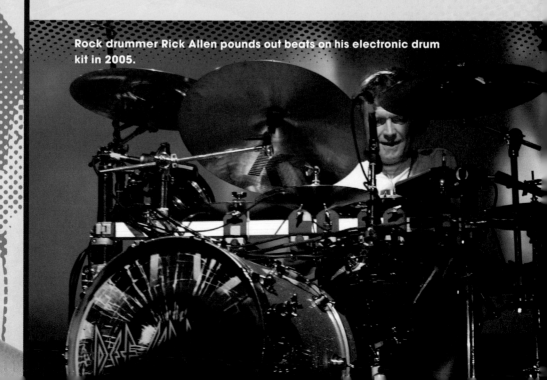

Rock drummer Rick Allen pounds out beats on his electronic drum kit in 2005.

Ringo pounds out the beat for the Beatles in 1965.

Do you enjoy the music of the British band the Beatles? Ringo Starr put the beat in most Beatles songs. Ringo's real name is Richard Starkey. He took the name Ringo Starr as a young musician because he often wore rings on his fingers. He thought the name made him sound like a cowboy too.

Ringo was sometimes called the funny Beatle. But he brought more than a sense of humor to the band. The Beatles played many different styles of music. Ringo was always able to find the right rhythm for a song. Ringo has a unique voice to match his drumming ability. You can hear him sing on popular Beatles songs such as "Yellow Submarine" and "Octopus Garden."

Does being a rock drummer appeal to you? If so, find the rock groups you like best and listen carefully to them. Pay special attention to the drummers. They might move you to take up the drums.

LOVE THAT JAZZ

What if rock isn't your thing? Maybe you're a jazz fan instead. Jazz drummers do more than set the groove for their music. The loose structure of jazz lets them add their own feelings and style.

Everyone knows that singing superstar Beyoncé Knowles is an outstanding performer. But did you know that she tours with two drummers who are outstanding in their own right? The drummers are Kim Thompson and Nikki Glaspie. They play in Suga Mama, Beyoncé's band (below, in 2009).

Thompson and Glaspie make Beyoncé's music bounce. They've been with the band since 2006, when Suga Mama formed. Both performers bring style and rhythm to Beyoncé's shows. If you get to see Beyoncé perform in person, Thompson and Glaspie will get you dancing!

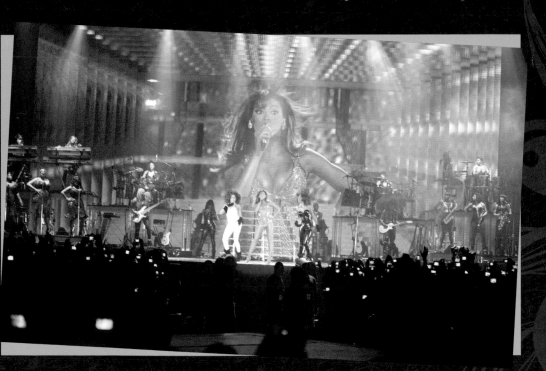

Drummer Buddy Rich became a legend in the jazz world. Rich toured with some of the most popular jazz musicians in the United States, including Tommy Dorsey and Harry James. He also played for the United Kingdom's Queen Elizabeth II as well as for U.S. presidents Franklin D. Roosevelt and John F. Kennedy.

Art Blakey was another famous jazz drummer. Blakey played a fast-paced, complex style of jazz called bebop. His first instrument was the piano, but the drums made him a legend. Blakey's bluesy but powerful playing inspired young drummers for years to come.

If you want to be a jazz drummer, don't limit yourself to the latest groups. You can pick up a lot from older bands as well. Keep an ear out for the drummer's sound. See if you can pick out different styles among these musicians. Think about whom you'd want to sound like.

Jazz legend Art Blakey warms up for a performance in 1971.

Steel drums—also known as steelpans—were invented in the Caribbean islands of Trinidad and Tobago. In the past, drum makers pounded out the bottom of an oil drum into a bowl to make a steelpan. More recently, they've used sheet metal instead. Drum makers press multiple grooves into the pan's surface. A player strikes these sections with a mallet, a thin stick with a large wooden head, to play different notes.

A typical steel drum band includes several different-sized steel drums. Each of these instruments has its own range of notes. When played together, the drums create a rich, textured sound.

Steelpan music has really caught on in recent years. Lessons are available in various cities. Some schools even have steel drum bands. Could this be your kind of drumming?

The members of this Tobago steel drum band make sweet music together.

CLASSICAL STYLE

Not everyone wants to be a rock or jazz drummer. Maybe you long to play the drums in a classical orchestra instead. If that's the case, you'll need to learn to play quite a few percussion instruments beyond a five-piece set. Percussionists in orchestras may be expected to play as many as forty instruments!

The xylophone and the triangle are used in all kinds of orchestras. Did you play one of these instruments when you were little? They are two of the first instruments many kids get their hands on. You may not even think of them as real instruments. But there's more to making music with a triangle

Classical percussionists have to be creative. Sometimes they use unusual items to get the right sound. "A classical music percussionist has to produce the sound the orchestra conductor wants," explained percussionist Guy St. Amant. "In one concert, I had a sheet of glass, and at the end of the piece, I would take a hammer and break the glass. In this case, the glass and the hammer became a percussion instrument."

or a xylophone than you might think. As Guy St. Amant explained, "You can hit any of these instruments and they'll make a sound. But to get them to speak the way you want them to speak is a learned skill." If you want a seat in the percussion section of an orchestra one day, learn as much as you can about all kinds of percussion instruments.

The marimba looks and sounds like a xylophone. It is made up of a set of wooden bars on a frame or a stand. You play the marimba by striking the bars with a mallet. The marimba has a warm, mellow tone that makes it great for Latin music. But it is also used in orchestras. Marimba players are the rock stars of classical percussion. They perform solos of their own. A marimba soloist might play with as many as six mallets at once!

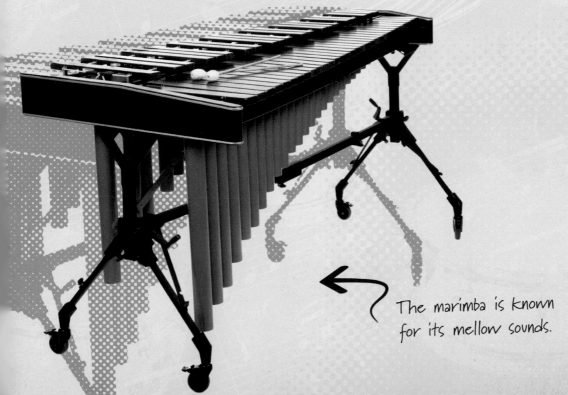

The marimba is known for its mellow sounds.

Drums have a long history. Small drums from as early as 3000 B.C. have been uncovered in caves. According to drummer Preston Ritter, drums are special because they were among the first musical instruments invented. "They are mentioned in the Bible and have been used by all cultures around the world since ancient times," Ritter noted.

Many cultures have used drums to communicate. "In Africa, drums were used to send long-distance messages from tribe to tribe," said Ritter. "Here in the United States, during the Civil War [1861–1865], drums were used to signal the troops to get ready for battle and for marching. Drums were even used during battle to give directions to the troops from their commanding officers."

Evelyn Glennie is a Grammy-winning percussionist who has played with orchestras throughout the world. She is also a successful solo performer. Glennie plays more than sixty different percussion instruments, such as the marimba, cymbals, and more. Glennie lost most of her hearing at a young age, but that hasn't stopped her from making great music. She learned to tell the pitch of a sound by what part of her body senses the vibration (the back-and-forth movement). Oftentimes, Glennie plays her music barefoot during concerts. This helps her to feel the music.

It doesn't matter what style of music you like best. You'll find that drums and other percussion instruments have a role in nearly all types of music. These instruments are the gateway to a rich world of sound and rhythm.

Evelyn Glennie performs a percussion solo with the BBC Orchestra in London, England, in 2007.

THREE

I WANNA PLAY! I WANNA PLAY!

Does this sound like you? You drum on kitchen pots and pans. You beat out rhythms on couches and pillows. You tap your fingers on tabletops. If you do these things, you may be on your way to becoming a real drummer.

Becoming a drummer is a fine goal, but how do you get started? People come to play the drums in many different ways. Let's look at how some professional drummers got their start.

OFF TO AN EARLY START

Many drummers start playing young. Some claim that they were born to play the drums.

20

Drummer Preston Ritter loved drumming from a very early age. He described what getting started was like for him. "When I was about five, I tied a pot around my neck with a string," Ritter recalled. "I used wooden spoons for drumsticks. I'd march around my block beating on a pot like a marching drum. I got my first real drum when I was thirteen."

How do you feel when you hear Latin music? Does it make you want to get up and dance? If so, you might want to play the bongo drums. Bongos are made up of two drums joined at the middle. One drum is always bigger than the other. To play these drums, you strike them with your palms and fingers.

Bongo drums have a clear, high-pitched sound. They can usually be heard over other instruments. They are easy to carry, and they don't cost too much. You don't even need drumsticks. Are these drums for you?

Steel drum musician Dexter Browne also started young. He spent his boyhood in Trinidad, where the steel drum is quite popular.

"Many steel drum music contests are held in Trinidad," Browne explained. "I was drawn to the sweet sound that came out of the instrument. Fortunately, my uncle was a steel drum musician. He agreed to teach me. By the time I was eleven, I could play along with him."

Young musicians play together at a steel drum festival in Trinidad.

A FRIEND WITH DRUMS IS A FRIEND INDEED

Sometimes young people are drawn into the music world because of their friends. That's how it was for drummer Philip Imperial. He described his experience this way:

> Some friends of mine started a band. I'd listen to them after school and help the drummer set up his drums. I spent a lot of time with him, and he taught me how to play.
>
> One night the drummer got sick and couldn't do a show. The band needed someone to fill in for him. The guys told me to take his place. I felt really scared. It was the first time I ever played in front of an audience.
>
> (But the performance went fine), and soon after that, my drummer friend had to leave the band. His grades had really dropped. The others in the band asked me to take his place, and I did. It turned out to be the start of my music career.

Do any of your friends already play the drums? You can learn a lot from other drummers. They might even let you try out their drum set.

Would you like to play a drum shaped like a great big soup kettle? If so, you might be interested in timpani (also known as kettle drums). In early times, these drums were used by the military. Later on, they were played in orchestras. Even rock drummers like timpani's booming sound. Timpani can be heard on some recordings by groups such as the Beatles, the Beach Boys, and Queen.

Timpani make some of the biggest sounds around.

MORE FORMAL LESSONS

Sooner or later, most musicians get some formal training. While there are other ways to learn, taking formal lessons can't hurt. It can only improve your musical skills.

Some students take private lessons with local teachers. Community centers sometimes offer drum lessons as well. These centers often have practice times when professional drummers are there to help you. Still other students enroll in the music programs at their schools. Many school programs will not have a drum set for beginners to use. Students who are interested in percussion instruments may start out on a set of bells or a single snare drum.

The right teacher can make a big difference in a young musician's future. That was true for percussionist Jeannine Maddox.

"I've always been drawn to music and always wanted to play an instrument," Maddox explained. "I started on the recorder, went on to the guitar, and finally found percussion. I also had a wonderful teacher and mentor who showed me where to get even better instruction. That teacher steered me toward studying at a conservatory (school of music)."

Many future drummers start out in school music programs or marching bands.

Most drums are made up of three basic parts. The body, or shell, of the drum gives the instrument its shape. The drum's shell can be any size or color. Drum shells are made out of different materials.

The top of the drum, or drumhead, is the thin piece of plastic or animal skin stretched across the shell. When you strike a drum, the drumhead vibrates. The sound the vibration creates travels through the drum's shell. This causes the shell to vibrate, making the sound even louder. The parts used to hold the drumhead and the shell together are called hardware. Hardware can include tacks, nails, bolts, or other fasteners.

Taken apart, the drum is a very simple instrument. But when played, it can be a powerhouse of sound.

A drum's three basic parts are its shell, its drumhead, and its hardware.

MAKING A DREAM COME TRUE

Lots of young people dream of being great drummers. Yet for many of them, it remains only a dream. They may take a few lessons and give up. So what makes some people stop while others succeed? Maybe Jeannine Maddox has the answer. As she noted, "You just have to want to do it. Playing your instrument must bring you joy!"

Does playing the drums bring you joy? If so, you've probably chosen the right instrument. And who knows? Someday you may be playing onstage with the best of them!

Do you dream about the drums?

FOUR

WHAT DO YOU NEED TO PLAY THE DRUMS?

True or false: Truly great drummers don't need training or practice. They are born with what it takes.

The answer to this question is definitely false. Some people may learn to play an instrument more easily than others. But if they don't work hard to develop their talent, they won't get very far.

Hard work is the key to drumming fun.

STICK WITH YOUR DRUMSTICKS

Time and effort are needed to learn to play an instrument well. The more you practice, the better you'll get. While practicing, try to always stay on track and think about what you're doing. And remember: fifteen or twenty minutes of daily practice is better than three or four hours the night before your music lesson.

Hard work and determination are the keys to success in music. At first, you might not like how you sound. That can be discouraging, but don't give up. In time, you'll improve.

"The first few months of learning a new instrument are the hardest," steel drum player Dexter Browne explained. "You're either going to stick with it, or you're going to quit. If you stick with it, you'll probably do well."

Playing the drums can be a challenge, but you will improve with practice.

HOW MANY HOURS OF PRACTICE DOES IT TAKE TO BECOME REALLY GOOD?

An expert drummer never stops learning. As drummer Seth Matthew Faulk noted, "They say it takes 10,000 hours of practice to master anything, but even the greatest of the greats will tell you there's always something more to learn."

PLAY WELL WITH OTHERS

There's more to being a successful musician than just playing well. You also need good people skills. It's important to get along well with others. Few drummers and percussionists play alone. You'll likely be playing in a band or an orchestra.

Musicians need to be team players. Be on time for practice sessions. Be sure you know your part well. Also be aware of the other musicians' needs and feelings. Don't demand star treatment for yourself. You may have talent, but there are many talented musicians. If you can't get along with others, you're probably not going to be asked to play with many groups.

"Music is, and always will be, a group effort," percussionist Jeff Handel said. "Even the greatest soloists must sometimes work with an accompanist. Music is almost as much about relationships as it is about sound."

As a drummer, you will need to work as part of a group.

John "Bonzo" Bonham was the drummer for British rock group Led Zeppelin. Bonzo developed a hard-hitting style that was all his own. He used the longest and heaviest drumsticks he could find. He even used to call his sticks "trees." In concert Bonham's drum solo during the song "Moby Dick" could last as long as a half hour.

KEEP YOUR COOL

Musicians have to work under all kinds of conditions. Things don't always go smoothly during a show. Lots of unsettling things can happen onstage. Sticks break, cymbals crack, and pedals and snares snap. The hardware on your drum might even fall apart.

It's also likely that sooner or later, you'll miss a note. If that happens,

Cymbals can crack during a performance.

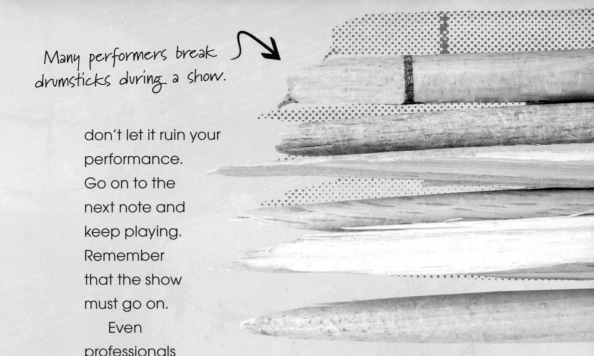

Many performers break drumsticks during a show.

don't let it ruin your performance. Go on to the next note and keep playing. Remember that the show must go on.

Even professionals make mistakes. Percussionist Jeff Handel recalled what once happened to him onstage:

I was playing a solo on the xylophone during a performance. I was using two mallets to play it, and at one point, I played a glissando (where you quickly hit all notes from lowest to highest). I accidentally hit one of my mallets out of my hand. The mallet flew 20 to 30 feet (6 to 9 meters) across the stage. I needed another mallet to continue my solo, so I had to walk back to my drum set, pick up another mallet, and walk back to the front of the stage to continue my solo. But I finished the solo, and everyone applauded. The craziest thing was that after the show, many people asked me if I meant to drop the mallet, and if I did that at every performance! They said they loved it!

Good drummers have to be ready for anything. A performer must be able to take things in stride. Here's what happened when Preston Ritter got caught in a tight spot:

[In my group], the drums were placed on top of a stage that was four or five feet [1.2 to 1.5 m] higher than the other musicians. [In one particular performance], my drum set was put on a stage that was actually two platforms that were joined together. As we were playing, I noticed that the two platforms were starting to separate. The crack between the platforms started out small but kept getting bigger. Then as we were playing our last song, the space got so large that my drum set fell into the crack, and I fell over backwards off the platform. I just disappeared suddenly in the middle of a song!

I was so embarrassed I didn't know if I should get back up or just stay hidden from the audience behind the drum platform. I decided to stand up and keep playing. The audience cheered when they saw me get back up and go on. I was happy that nothing was injured but my pride that night.

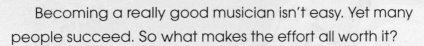

Becoming a really good musician isn't easy. Yet many people succeed. So what makes the effort all worth it?

For most musicians, their love of music is the key. If you really love what you're doing, practice doesn't feel like punishment. You want to spend all your spare time on your drums or other percussion instruments. Drummer Seth Matthew Faulk described it this way: "I became a musician because there is nothing else in the world that makes me feel more excited, creative, or fulfilled. I became a musician because I am in love with music."

Is that how you feel about your music? Are you willing to do what you need to be an outstanding musician? If so, you're on the track to success.

QUIZ: ARE THE DRUMS RIGHT FOR YOU?

Which of these statements describes you best? Please record your answers on a separate sheet of paper.

1. **If at first you don't succeed,**
   - **A.** You try, try again. You like to finish what you start. People say you're the determined type.
   - **B.** You feel that a lack of success means it wasn't meant to be. You prefer to try something else that you may be better at.

2. **When you hear a good piece of music,**
   - **A.** You get really into all the sounds. You feel as if you could listen to the piece forever!
   - **B.** You think it sounds good, but you don't usually get too absorbed in it. You'd rather spend time working on art or learning new soccer moves than listening closely to music.

3. **When it's time to dance,**
   - **A.** You can move to the beat. Your timing is the best.
   - **B.** You often step on your partner's feet. Rhythm has never been one of your strong points.

4. **When you're working toward a long-term goal,**
   - **A.** You tend to be patient. Practicing a skill again and again doesn't bother you.
   - **B.** You get a little antsy. You'd rather move on to something new than focus on the same task for a long time.

5. **When you think about practicing your instrument,**
   - **A.** You get really excited. You think studying an instrument sounds like fun!
   - **B.** You like music, but you can think of other things you'd rather do. Giving up free time to practice every day doesn't sound worth it.

Were your answers mostly A's?

If so, the drums may just be the right choice for you!

GLOSSARY

bass drum: a large drum with a deep, low sound

cymbal: a brass or bronze plate that produces a ringing sound when struck

five-piece set: the type of drum set most commonly used in rock and jazz music

hi-hat: a pair of cymbals in which one faces up while the other faces down. The two are pushed together when the drummer steps on a pedal.

jazz: a form of music characterized by loose structure and improvisation

mallet: a stick with a wooden head used to play some percussion instruments

percussion family: a group of instruments that makes a sound when they are struck or shaken

pitch: the highness or lowness of a sound

snare drum: a shallow drum with a set of wires called a snare stretched across its bottom

solo: a musical performance in which a performer plays alone

tom-tom: a drum without a snare that is often part of a five-piece set

SOURCE NOTES

6   Jeff Handel, e-mail message to author, July 18, 2009.
16   Guy St. Amant, interview with author, July 19, 2009.
17   Ibid.
18   Preston Ritter, e-mail message to author, June 4, 2009.
21   Ibid.
22   Dexter Browne, telephone conversation with author, July 23, 2009.
23   Philip Imperial, interview with author, July 9, 2009.
25   Jeannine Maddox, e-mail message to author, June 7, 2009.
27   Ibid.
29   Browne.

30 Seth Matthew Faulk, e-mail message to author, July 14, 2009.
31 Handel.
33 Ibid.
34 Ritter.
35 Faulk.

SELECTED BIBLIOGRAPHY

Benade, Arthur H. *Fundamentals of Musical Acoustics*. 2nd ed. Mineola, NY: Dover Publications, 1990.

Stevens, Christine. *The Art and Heart of Drum Circles*. Milwaukee: Hal Leonard, 2003.

Strong, Jeff. *Drums for Dummies*. 2nd ed. Hoboken, NJ: Wiley, 2006.

Waring, Dennis. *Making Drums*. New York: Sterling, 2003.

FOR MORE INFORMATION

Bootman, Colin. *The Steel Pan Man of Harlem*. Minneapolis: Carolrhoda Books, 2009. This book retells the legend of the Pied Piper—of Harlem instead of Hamlin—with colorful illustrations and a Caribbean drumming twist.

Drums and Percussion
http://www.rhythmweb.com/kids/index.html
Visit this website to see how kids enjoy drums around the world. The site also lets you listen to music you can practice along with and features a craft page that shows you how to make a drum.

Fyffe, Daniel. *Indoor Percussion Ensembles and Drum Corps*. New York: Rosen, 2007. Young readers wanting to know the basics about participating in marching band percussion activities will find it in this book. Information on how to get involved in drum corps is supplied too.

Kenney, Karen Latchana. *Cool Rock Music: Create and Appreciate What Makes Music Great!* Edina, MN: Abdo, 2008. This book introduces rock music and the instruments used to play it. There's also info on writing a rock song and making a rock video.

THE DRUMMERS AND PERCUSSIONISTS WHO HELPED WITH THIS BOOK

This book could not have been written without the great insights of these drummers and percussionists.

DEXTER BROWNE
Dexter Browne is a steel drum musician who started the reggae-calypso band Pan Paradise.

SETH MATTHEW FAULK
Seth Matthew Faulk has played the drums with many groups ranging from oldies bands to heavy metal groups to the indie rock band Fire Flies.

JEFF HANDEL
Jeff Handel is the percussionist for the group the Dallas Brass. He is also a music educator.

PHILIP IMPERIAL
Philip Imperial has played the drums and the percussion in orchestras in both the United States and the Philippines. He is a drummer with Celebrity Cruises.

JEANNINE MADDOX
Jeannine Maddox is a marimba player and director of instrumental music at Westtown School in Westtown, Pennsylvania.

REY MONROIG
Rey Monroig is a drummer and a music educator in the Miami, Florida, area.

ADAM NUSSBAUM
Adam Nussbaum has played with the jazz great Stan Getz. Nussbaum is a member of the Nuttree Quartet.

GUY ST. AMANT
Guy St. Amant was formerly the principal percussionist for the Florida Philharmonic Orchestra.

DARCEY TIMMERMAN
Darcey Timmerman is a percussionist with the Malaysian Philharmonic Orchestra.

INDEX

PHOTO ACKNOWLEDGMENTS

The images in this book are used with the permission of: © iStockphoto.com/Andresr, p. 1; © Sheftsoff/Dreamstime.com, p. 3; © altrendo images/Getty Images, pp. 4, 31; AP Photo/CP, Nunatsiaq News-Chris Windeyer, p. 5; © iStockphoto.com/Elena Schweitzer, p. 6; © James Woodson/Getty Images, p. 7; © Perkus/Dreamstime.com, pp. 8–9, 27; © Monkeybusinessimages/Dreamstime.com, pp. 10–11; AP Photo/Robert E. Klein, p. 11; © Michael Ochs Archives/Getty Images, p. 12; © Tom Daskalakis/IML Image Group, p. 13; © Lebrecht Music and Arts Photo Library/Alamy, p. 14; © ImageState/Alamy, p. 15; © iStockphoto.com/Michael Flippo, p. 17; © North Wind Picture Archives/Alamy, p. 18; © Chris Christodoulou/Lebrecht Music & Arts, p. 19; © SuperStock RF/SuperStock, p. 20; © Maspi/Dreamstime.com, p. 21; © Robert Harding Picture Library Ltd/Alamy, p. 22; © iStockphoto.com/Bart Coenders, p. 23; © Dorling Kindersley/Getty Images, p. 24; © Khabar/Dreamstime.com, p. 25; © iStockphoto.com/Ju-Lee, p. 26; © Digital Vision/Getty Images, p. 28; © Somos Images/Alamy, p. 29; © iStockphoto.com/Arthur Carlo Franco, p. 30; © iStockphoto.com/Ernesto Rolandelli, p. 32; © Vlue/Dreamstime.com, p. 33; © Rayman/Getty Images, p. 35.

Front Cover: © iStockphoto.com/Andresr.